The Grey Gr
Pres ay

AHHH...

COLLEAGUES!

AN ILLUSTRATED COLLECTION OF
CONFOUNDING COWORKERS

BY

PROFESSOR E. DIOTBüRGER

www.greygreyeveryday.com

ISBN: 978-1-0369-3137-7

Disclaimer

Although these characters may feel familiar, this is a work of fiction. All characters, names, places, and situations are either entirely imaginary or exaggerated beyond recognition for comedic effect. Any resemblance to actual persons, living or dead, or real places is purely coincidental.

If you think one of these characters is you, maybe it's time for some self-reflection—or a coffee break. As for the settings, let's be honest, all offices look the same.

INTRODUCTION

This monograph is a pictorial account of an intrepid expedition I took into the world of 'work'. Whilst exploring this delicate ecosystem, I observed and analysed those who engage in its employment.

My findings lead me to postulate that the same personages can be found in all 'workplaces', with the only variations being moniker, occupation, and/or odour.

Additionally, I theorise that all individuals, despite their differing attributes, fall into one of two categories. Although both groups are in a constant state of flux, they share one consistent commonality (see Fig. 1).

Using a combination of spurious, empirical accounts and evidence, I conducted a character study and compiled this compendium of 'colleagues'. My aim: to illuminate, educate and hopefully help others navigate this ubiquitous undertaking.

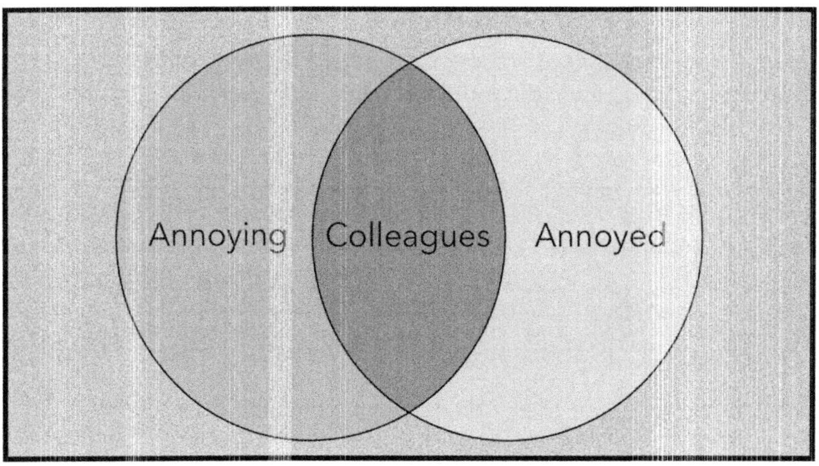

Fig. 1.

'YA KNOW WHAT I MEAN' JANINE

Not content with delaying their own duties, these individuals seek to encumber all with celebrity confab and insipid opinions.

Classification: *Inhibentes Aliis*

Reception
The Corporate
Nonsense Awards
Efficiency in
Services
Customer
Award

ARTIE FACT

A rare relic of workplace antiquity.

Classification: *Fossile Decrepitum*

Depreciated
Assets
Archived
Archived

BUZZING BARBARA

After several palpitation-inducing drinks, they're sharp as a knife. Sadly, the team must walk on that knife's edge for the rest of the day.

The question is, what came first, the caffeine or the collywobbles?

Classification: *Eruptio Imminenti*

JIM GUY

As they inappropriately extrude their meaty limbs into your personal space and call it callisthenics, you recoil. Partly because of the shameful contrast between your life choices. Mostly because you've just realised: those aren't tight clothes, it's body paint.

Classification: *Virili Escam Massa*

TABITHA TANTRUM

It's their way or you'll hear about it all day.

Classification: *Adultus Puerilis*

I am a
Big Girl

KOMBUCHA KEVIN

These self-appointed foodies live to impart the latest masticatory marvels and make their counterparts feel less cultured than a starter yeast. From charcuterie to civet coffee, if it's not fermented, forget it!

Classification: *Pompous Palatum*

Fermented
DAILY MEOW

JURASSIC MARK

They say age is just a number... unless you predate numbers.

Classification: *Ante Historia*

Modernisatio
HISTORIC DATA

CODY MORSE

A digit drumming, keyboard clobbering, cup clanking, pen tapping, stapling sadist. Either that, or they're a devious double agent selling the world's dullest secrets.

Classification: *Irritatio Percussiva*

Info
Rep
Ads
Code
Data
Coding Data
operation
snooze fest

MAYA MOUTH-BREATHER

An idiosyncrasy so annoying that it both sucks and blows in equal measures.

Classification: *Involuntarium Insectivori*

WED
THURS
FRI
Colour
Print
Scan
Copy

THE GIANT

Fitting in at work can be difficult, especially for these monolithic members of the team.

Classification: *Colossicus Humano*

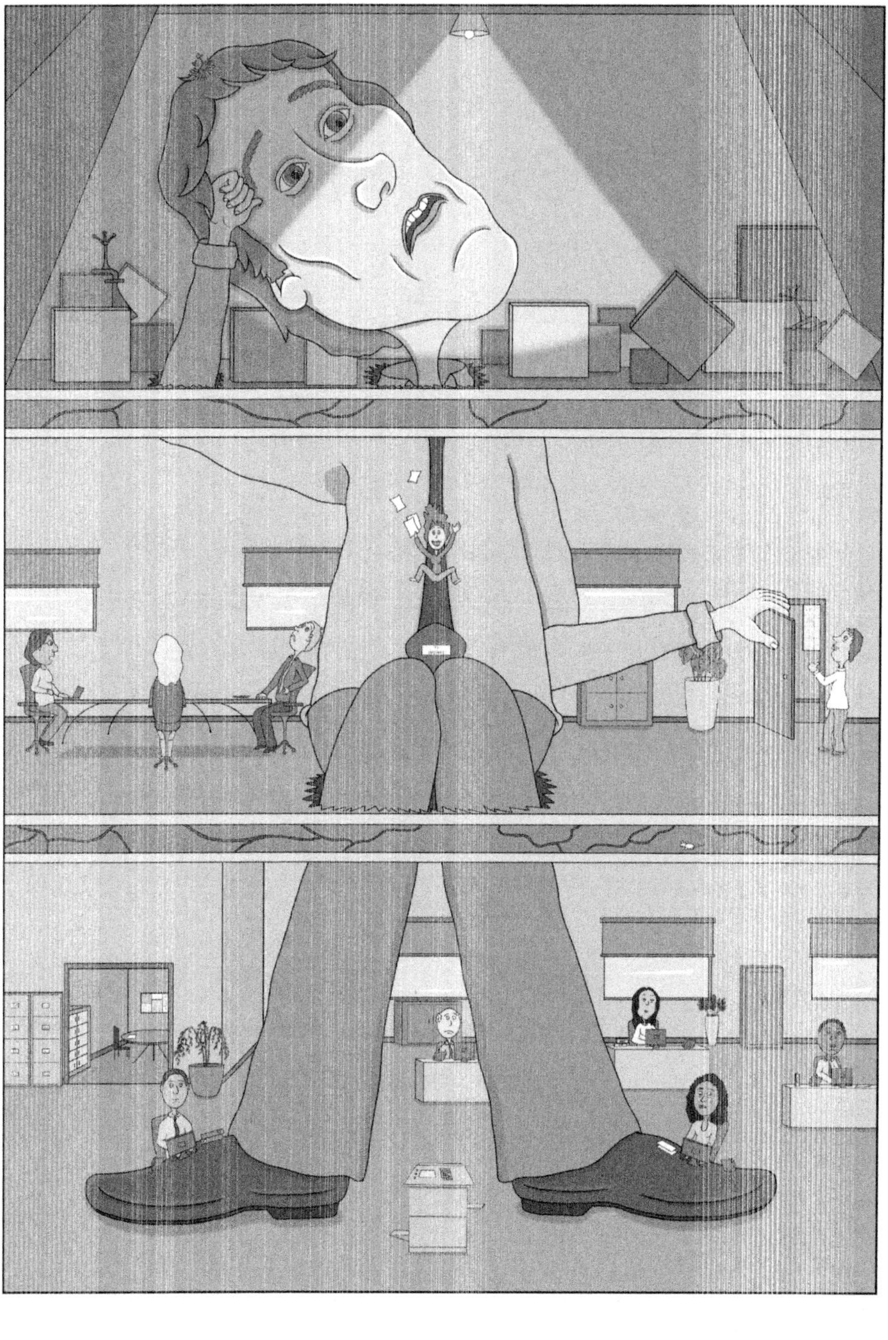

MICHELLE MEETIN

Their constant desire to conduct conclaves causes a conundrum: they hold more congregations than they have content to fill them. Booking meetings to discuss previous meetings and or to arrange future meetings, they leave you screaming to get off their dizzying merry-go-round of minutes.

Classification: *Carcer Infinitus Conventuum*

SAME-BOAT BRETT

This figurehead is always on hand to chip in—morally that is. Sure, there's no I in team, but there is in otiose, entitled and dividend.

'We're all in this together'
– Someone who definitely isn't in it with you –

Classification: *Tutum Commodum*

BOSSIN' IT

GROUNDHOG GLENDA

Repetitive rambling is the secret weapon of these time-tampering theurgists. A colleague can easily be pulled into their verbose vortices and waste a lifetime trapped in a loop of wishy-washy waffle.

Classification: *Taediosus Repetita Personam*

Best
Office Space
Award
P/O
Ref

AL LIEN

Albeit an upstanding exemplar of colleaguism, there's just something about them that you can't put your finger on...

Classification: *Organismus Incognitus*

PHONE HOME
Expense Taxes
Unsolved Accounts

'SORRY I'M LATE' SIMON

A remorseful recidivist who, despite delay, inexplicably finds time to procure refreshment en route. If only they were as punctual as they are partial to a latte.

Classification: *Semper Sero*

EXIT
TIME SHEETS
TIME SHEETS

ANNE APOTHECARY

Full of 'zenergy', these happy, holistic hippies believe there's nothing crystals can't cure (although management disagrees).

Classification: *Spiritus Liberum*

Make love
Not paperwork

BUFFERING BOB

If a swift reboot up the base unit doesn't work,
it might be time to pull the plug...

Classification: *Contritum Cerebrum*

Getting to the point
JENNY
RAY
KIM
BEN
Consciousness
Loading...
Archives
BCE

KELLY KLAXON

If they're here, you'll hear.

Classification: *Magnus Oris*

Corporate
Nonsense Award
For
Communications

TOXIC TOM

Some say the grind has gotten to them, others insist it's inherent. Perhaps it's years of sitting next to the old copier that the boss is too cheap to replace. As the nature-nurture debate continues, be sure to protect yourself against these poisonous personae.

Classification: *Diffundit Tristiti*

FALLOUT
ZONE

UNSEEMLY ELLIE

Putting a blazer on does not automatically make any attire ‘work appropriate’.

Classification: *Nimis Denudo*

CENSORED
CENSORED

THE SUCK UP

Brace your backend because there's no stopping these sycophantic subservients.

Classification: *Oscula Asinum*

Boss
Pro
Suck

VIV ARIUM

A gifted green-fingered grower who takes great pride in their plants. However, it's undetermined if their botanical barricade is deliberate or if things have simply gotten out of hand.

Classification: *Infestus Hortus*

The Corporate
onsense Awards
Winner Of The
usiness Growth
Award
A-F
G-O
P-U

BARNEY BRAGG

Out-of-office officials are commonly known as "OOO." Sounded spectrally, it reflects their presence—felt only in spirit. Alternatively, it's pronounced with ironic awe, mimicking the polite noise you make as you feign interest in their latest corporate jolly... whilst you work late. Again.

Classification: *Retro Sedilum Gloria*

Hard Work Pays Dividends
Ad Hoc
Ad Hoc
Ad Hoc
Ad Hoc
Ad Hoc
Ad Hoc
Ad Hoc
14-104

WHO DUNG IT?

Numerous failed flushes and splatter-cast crimes mean a mystery is afoot. The ordure and method of deposit are so unique, there's only one conclusion: you have a monster in your midst. Instantly, a few suspects will spring to mind, but remember, remain vigilant, the faecal felon could be anyone...

Classification: *Clandéstinis Excrementus Spargium*

Perpetual Office Offences Squad
SUSPECT: SHORT DERRICK
DEPT: WAREHOUSE
Perpetual Office Offences Squad
SUSPECT: LANKY ERIC
DEPT: SALES
Perpetual Office Offences Squad
SUSPECT: SANDRA
DEPT: ADMIN

GAS, GAS, GAS GAIL

Every day, the contents of their Tupperware strikes terror into the team's nostrils.

Classification: *Inconsideratus Comedenti*

CREEPING CARMICHAEL

No matter the time or place, should you zone out for even a second, these shadowy wraiths will be there to scare you soulless.

Classification: *Occultus Daemontus*

THELMA STAT

Climate change is a contentious topic both politically and professionally.

Classification: *Contra Temperatus*

SAM SICKDAE

They say absence makes the heart grow fonder. However, these medical marvels have so much time off, their very existence is but a canard to their compeers.

Classification: *Asserta Infirmum*

B S
• Crumpled Klinem
• Rinky Dink Fever
• Collapsed Prapple
• Nautical Prinkles
• Fractured Anus
• Pippins Collium
• Stanklemans Lift
• Hyperbolic Mosaic
• Greedy Septum
• Richmonds Crink
• Trapped Klondike
• Sniffles
• Fleckenhofferhiem

MICROWAVE MICKY

Behold, the colleagues of the future! Inaction and radiation will see microwave messes become sentient. The good news: work is all they know, so they'll be committed members of the team. The bad news: even they're more likely to get promoted than you. Hurry—there's still time...

Classification: *Per Ordines Radians*

NATHAN NEWBIE

Clearly, this person lied on their curriculum vitae. If you're going to fake it until you make it, try to be a little convincing along the way.

Classification: *Fictiti Experienco*

Professional Integrity Award
No:174
Sales
Out
A/26
Index
Co: 74
DIN
Left
Rota
Dept

YAZ 'SO' MEAN

You will never see eye to eye with this modern-day Medusa, and nor would you want to. Their unprovoked, stone-cold, bombastic side eye can obliterate anyone within a thirty-foot range.

Classification: *Oculus Malus*

NOAH BODY-KNOWES

This dope thinks their recreational activities go under the radar when actually, they fly high, really high, above it!

Classification: *Etiamnum Alto*

XII
III
VI
IX

OVERSHARER SARAH

Despite your best effort not to, you know everything about this person. Unbosoming to any ear, uncle's affairs and third cousin's third mammary papilla are par for the course in their open therapy sessions.

Classification: *Nimia Informatio*

MANNY GAIMES

Great quantities of gubbins fill their workspaces in some form of abstract Feng Shui. Sadly, collecting isn't a substitute for charisma. Most colleagues have hobbies, but they just choose to leave them at home!

Classification: *Immaturitio Accumulus*

T.O.Y.S

TORNADO TINA

A force to be reckoned with, these highly motivated individuals consider themselves the backbone of the team. With great gusto, they attempt to take on every task alone, even if that means ruffling their fellows.

Classification: *Formidabilis Tempestas*

Marketing
Warehouse
Finance

OBLIGATORY BABY

Though not technically a colleague, the inconvenience of these invading infants and the length of their stay can certainly make it feel that way.

Classification: *Parva Vomitus Hospes*

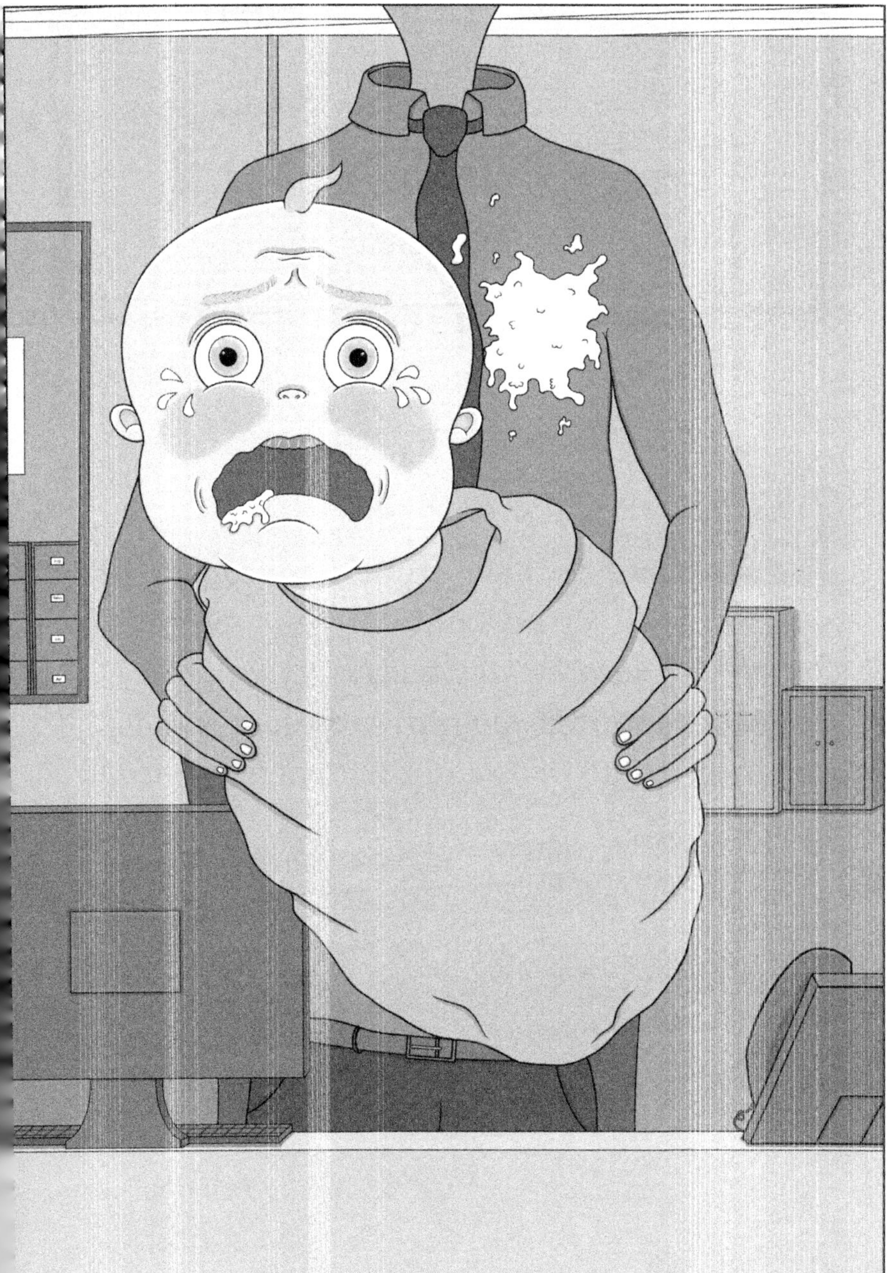

THE FOOD STEALER

The effects of these cryptid colleagues are widely felt, yet no sightings have ever been confirmed. However, it's believed that with every misappropriated mouthful, these gluttonous goblins grow as physically unappealing as their principles.

Classification: *Porcus Bestia Fur*

Tea

FAYE FUNDAE

Horrible homemade cakes, embarrassing attire and extroverted activities; they see every day as an opportunity for an event. Seemingly never doing any work, you wonder if they've donated their desks to their cause. To date, the company's biggest charitable contribution is that these individuals are still employed.

Classification: *Opusi Fugax*

Workplace Nonsense Fund
Fun Run
1076
13
86

EBENEZER GEEZER

Camouflaging their superiority by adopting colleague colloquialisms, you think this commander is just like you. That is, until they reject your reasonable request for an increase in line with inflation, whilst rolling away in their Rolls-Royce.

Classification: *Iniustus Avarusia*

Geezer
irector

AMELIA EYREHEAD

By no means a high-flyer, yet they're always in the clouds. Needing constant help and attention, the amiability of these soft-headed individuals cancels out their incompetence (for most at least).

Classification: *Stultitus Amicus*

P-R
Ref
S-U
P/O
V-Z
Index
Co
Pins

CELEBRATION SHAKEDOWN SOCIETY

Everyone makes sacrifices at work, but some make it feel like attending the office costs you more than you're earning.

Classification: *Coactus Donatio*

HAPPY
BIRTHD
GIFT AID

DEATH-BREATH BREVIN

Friendly and always willing to help, but sadly, they're oblivious to their oral omissions. Wincing through the wretchedness, you'll get that pivot table done in a jiffy. However, they'll leave your lifeless corpse in their wake.

Classification: *Halitus Malus*

Safeguarding

CHILL-PILL JILL

Somnolent in their state of inertia, not a single furrow features on these carefree colleagues. Constantly telling you to 'relax' because 'everything will be ok', but you know it'll only be fine because you'll fix it!

Classification: *Alius Id Faciet*

LUNCHTIME LARRY

Exuberant to the point of exploding, this interpersonal peccadillo won't give you a moment's peace. Acting as if you are the first human they've seen in decades, consequently, they are both a sayer and a sprayer.

Classification: *Sonorus Prandium*

GABBY TELLSALL

This HR nightmare is a HR nightmare. They know everything and tell everyone.

Classification: *Infidelus Ad Secreta*

HR
Juicie
G-Sip
Private
HR Only
Confidential

DAN SLOBINSKI

The rules of maintaining one's workspace are unwritten. Therefore, inevitably, opinions on acceptable standards vary.

Classification: *Sordida Et Inordinata*

S.T-Inc
DI-RT
MUCK
DRANK

BANDWAGON BILLY

Jabbering juveniles, delinquent dabbers and callow cinnamon scoffers. Collectively, they are known as 'TikTokers' due to their time wasting. Following trends to make friends, they busk for affection and beg to be liked. In other words, total plankers.

Classification: *Attentionibus Cupidi*

THE ACCOUNTATRON 3000

Cold and calculating, they mean business, and errors will equal annihilation.

Classification: *Numero Machina Mortis*

ccounts

THE PARTY POOPER

They will do anything to bring the good vibes down... ANYTHING!

Classification: *Interfectorem Gaudii*

Congratulations Kate
DRANK
DRANK

Afterword

I hope this study serves you well during your own intrepid adventures in the world of 'work'. As thanks for your readership, I would like to bestow upon you the honour of contributing to this pivotal paper. Be it your own findings or a dedication, I welcome your addendum to the overleaf.

To quote an old proverb, 'It takes a village to raise a child,' or rather, in this instance, it takes a company to raise a colleague.

Onward ho, to the next ~~un~~known.
Yours in discovery,

Prof E. Diotbürger

Classification:

Printed in Dunstable, United Kingdom

71682966R00067